FALSE LOGIC PUZZLES

Norman D. Willis

Sterling Publishing Co., Inc.
New York

To Carol Willis Buechler.
Her ideas and critique contributed
importantly to this book.

Edited by Claire Bazinet

Library of Congress Cataloging-in-Publication Data

Willis, Norman D.
   False Logic Puzzles / Norman D. Willis.
        p.   cm.
   Includes index.
   ISBN 0-8069-9804-0
   1. Puzzles. 2. Logic I. Title.
   GV1493.W49655   1997
   793.73—dc21   96-29531
                                                       CIP

10 9 8 7

Published by Sterling Publishing Company, Inc.
387 Park Avenue South, New York, N.Y. 10016
© 1997 by Norman D. Willis
Distributed in Canada by Sterling Publishing
$^{c}/_{o}$ Canadian Manda Group, One Atlantic Avenue, Suite 105
Toronto, Ontario, Canada M6K 3E7
Distributed in Great Britain by Chrysalis Books
64 Brewery Road, London N7 9NT, England
Distributed in Australia by Capricorn Link (Australia) Pty, Ltd.
P.O. Box 704, Windsor, NSW 2756 Australia
Printed in China

Sterling ISBN 0-8069-9804-0

CONTENTS

Before You Begin

There are five different types of logic puzzles in this book. They have one particular thing in common—each contains at least one false statement, which must be identified in order to solve the puzzle.

In solving puzzles, it is important to follow a sound method of analysis, including trial and error. After all the alternatives in a puzzle are clear to you, assume that each one in turn is correct, and test each against the puzzle's considerations. Eliminate those assumptions that reveal inconsistencies or contradictions, and what remains is the solution. For most puzzles, use diagrams to aid in your analysis and in organizing tentative conclusions. Suggested diagrams are presented in both the Hints and Solutions sections. Also, the Solutions section contains considerations for solving the puzzles. These will be helpful in solving other puzzles of the same type.

The puzzles are grouped by type, and you will find a wide range of difficulty within each type. Those puzzles identified by one asterisk (*) are challenging yet capable of being successfully solved by the reader who approaches them conscientiously. It is recommended that in a particular section the puzzles marked by one asterisk be completed first. Those puzzles identified by two asterisks (**) are difficult and will be solved by experienced logic puzzle solvers. Those puzzles marked by three asterisks (***) are rated as very difficult and intended for only the most experienced solvers.

— 1 —

Socrates Lends a Hand

Socrates is credited with being the first known formal logic thinker. He devoted his life to expanding his knowledge, and helping others to do the same. His method was to employ a questioning technique using given propositions and arriving at answers by deductive reasoning. Since Socrates was known among his fellow Athenians as possessing great skill in analysis and deductive reasoning, he was frequently called upon to resolve disputes and to solve crimes.

Each of the puzzles in this section involves problems or crimes, and contains statements by individuals, some of which are true and some of which are false. To find the solutions it is necessary to determine which statements are false and which are not.

P1-1 Who Owns the Mule?*

Three farmers who have shared the use of a mule for some time disagree as to who owns the animal. It is not certain, however, that the responsibility of ownership is desired. They have asked Socrates to settle the issue. The three make the following statements. Each makes one true and one false statement.

- A. 1. It is C's mule.
  2. I can make no claim to it.
- B. 1. C has no right to it.
  2. It is A's mule.
- C. 1. It is my mule.
  2. B's second statement is false.

Socrates hesitates for scarcely an instant and determines the owner. To which farmer does the mule belong?

(Hints on page 43)

(Solution on page 53)

P1-2 Theft of Homer's Writings*

Valuable writings of Homer are missing. They have been stolen from the library in the Parthenon by one of three suspects. The three are questioned by Socrates, and each makes one true and two false statements, as follows:

- A. 1. I did not even know that Homer's books were in the Parthenon.
  2. C is innocent.
  3. B must be the thief.
- B. 1. I did not do it.
  2. A is innocent.
  3. A's first statement is true.

C. 1. Homer's writings are not worth taking.
   2. A did it; or else it was B.
   3. I would never consider such a dishonest thing.

Which one is guilty?

(Hints on page 43)
(Solution on page 53)

P1-3 Who Left the Cell Door Open?*

When Socrates was imprisoned for being a disturbing influence, he was held in high esteem by his guards. All four of them hoped that something would occur that would facilitate his escape. One evening, the guard who was on duty intentionally left the cell door open so that Socrates could leave for distant parts.

Socrates did not attempt to escape, as it was his philosophy that if you accept society's rules, you must also accept its punishments. However, the open door was considered by the authorities to be a serious matter. It is not clear which guard was on duty that evening. The four guards make the following statements in their defense:

A. 1. I did not leave the door open.
   2. C was the one who did it.
B. 1. I was not the one who was on duty that evening.
   2. A was on duty.
C. 1. B was the one who was on duty that evening.
   2. I hoped Socrates would escape.
D. 1. I did not leave the door open.
   2. I am not surprised that Socrates did not attempt to escape.

Considering that, in total, three statements are true, and five statements are false, which guard is guilty?

(Hints on page 43)
(Solution on page 54)

P1-4 A Secret Observer*

As Socrates' reputation grew, there were those who were jealous of his fame, and who had been embarrassed by his method of cross-examining to gain the truth. There was a movement to indict Socrates as a negative and disturbing influence. A citizen was chosen to secretly pose as a student of Socrates, to observe his teaching and gain evidence against him. Socrates was informed that one of four followers was, in reality, such an observer. Socrates questioned the four. Their statements follow. All statements are true except any mentioning the secret observer.

- A. 1. C is definitely a student, here to learn.
  - 2. D is a stranger to me.
- B. 1. A and D are not acquainted.
  - 2. C is not the observer.
- C. 1. B's first statement is false.
  - 2. A's second statement is true.
- D. 1. C's first statement is false.
  - 2. A's first statement is true.

Which of the four speakers is the observer?

(Hints on page 43)
(Solution on pages 54–55)

P1-5 Theft from the Statue of Athena*

A piece from the gold-and-ivory statue of Athena was stolen. There was evidence that the thief, acting alone, entered the temple in the dead of night and used a large hammer to dislodge a piece of the statue. Socrates agreed to cross-examine four suspects, all of whom were in Athens when the crime occurred. One of them is guilty. One suspect makes three true statements; one suspect makes three false statements. As to the truthfulness of the statements by the other two suspects, little is known. Their statements follow:

A. 1. I did not do it.
    2. I was in Philius when the crime occurred.
    3. B is guilty.
B. 1. I am innocent.
    2. C owns a large hammer.
    3. C was seen at the Acropolis late that night.
C. 1. I do not own a large hammer.
    2. A and B are both guilty.
    3. I went to bed early that night.
D. 1. Only one of my statements is false.
    2. C was out late that night.
    3. I am innocent.

Which one is the thief?

(Hints on page 43)
(Solution on page 55)

P1-6 Who Should Lead the Victory Parade?*

At the successful end of the war with Persia, it was decided that there should be a parade through the main streets of Athens. At the front of the procession should be the soldier who had led the charge during the last battle, but the identity of this soldier was unclear. Socrates was asked to decide who should lead the parade, and he questioned three candidates. One of them makes one false statement; one makes two false statements; one makes three false statements, as follows:

A. 1. I led the charge in the last battle.
   2. I am clearly the choice to lead the parade.
   3. C was in the reserve ranks during the battle.
B. 1. C did not lead the charge during the last battle.
   2. I am the logical choice to lead the parade.
   3. I could keep in time with the parade music very well.
C. 1. I should be selected.
   2. B would not be able to keep in time with the parade music.
   3. I was not in the reserve ranks during the last battle.

Which soldier should lead the parade?

(Hints on page 44)
(Solution on page 56)

P1-7 Socrates Plans a Trip*

Socrates wanted to take a trip to Philius, and decided that one of his young followers should accompany him. Three of them expressed keen interest, and Socrates questioned them to determine which one of the three should be selected.

The disciple selected makes three true or three false statements. Of the other two, one makes two true and one false statement, and one makes one true and two false statements. Their statements follow:

A. 1. C is the oldest.
   2. B would not carry the baggage.
   3. I am the one with three true statements.
B. 1. I would carry the baggage.
   2. C will be chosen.
   3. A's first statement is false.

C. 1. I am the oldest, so I should be selected.
   2. B will be selected.
   3. B's third statement is true.

Which follower did Socrates select to accompany him?

(Hints on page 44)
(Solution on pages 56–57)

P1-8 Who Should Repair the Statue?**

After the damage to the statue of Athena, Socrates was requested to select the most qualified craftsman to undertake the necessary repairs. He interviewed four recommended craftsmen. Their statements were not all truthful. However, each of the four makes the same number of true statements and the same number of false statements, as follows:

A. 1. I do not have all the necessary tools.
   2. D is the most qualified.
   3. C is experienced in this type of work.
B. 1. A is the most qualified.
   2. D has never worked with ivory.
   3. A's first statement is false.
C. 1. I am experienced in this type of work.
   2. B is the most qualified.
   3. A does not have all the necessary tools.
D. 1. C is the most qualified.
   2. A does not have all the necessary tools.
   3. I have never worked with ivory.

Which craftsman should Socrates select?

(Hints on page 44)
(Solution on pages 57–58)

P1-9 Who Won the Discus Throw?**

The Athenian Games involved several athletic events. Following the games one season, there was a dispute as to who had won the discus throw. Socrates agreed to question the competitors and determine the winner. The statements of four of the athletes are below. No two make the same number of false statements.

- A. 1. C did not win the discus throw.
  2. I was second.
  3. C and I trained together.
- B. 1. A was the winner.
  2. I placed a close second.
  3. C and I trained together.
- C. 1. B was the winner.
  2. I did not train with anyone.
  3. A was second.
- D. 1. A was not the winner.
  2. B was second.
  3. C and I trained together.

Who won the discus event?

(Hints on page 44)
(Solution on pages 58–59)

P1-10 The Food Produce Thief***

Five citizens were asked to deliver food to the Acropolis to provide a meal for city dignitaries who were meeting there. One delivered bread; one delivered goats' cheese; one delivered honey; one delivered milk; and one delivered nuts. Shortly after the produce was left, significant amounts of the food were found to be missing, illegally acquired, it was determined, by one of the five citizens.

Socrates agreed to cross-examine the suspects. Their statements are below. The one who delivered the milk makes three true statements; the one who delivered the cheese makes two true and one false statement; the one who delivered the honey makes one true and two false statements; and the one who delivered the bread and the one who delivered the nuts each makes three false statements.

A. 1. I did not deliver the bread.
   2. D is the one who stole the food.
   3. B delivered the honey.
B. 1. I did not deliver the cheese.
   2. I am certainly not guilty.
   3. C delivered the honey.
C. 1. I did not deliver the honey.
   2. B's second statement is false.
   3. D is not the thief.
D. 1. I did not deliver the nuts.
   2. A is the thief.
   3. E delivered the bread.
E. 1. I did not deliver the milk.
   2. C stole the food.
   3. A delivered the bread.

Which one delivered which food product, and who is guilty?

(Hints on page 44)
(Solution on pages 60–61)

P1-11 Theft at the Open Market***

A theft has occurred at the Athenian open market. A variety of goods has been stolen including a large quantity that would require a cart to transport.

Four suspects are questioned by Socrates and one of them is the culprit. The statements of the four are below. None of the suspects is completely truthful, and no two make the same number of true statements.

- A. 1. D has been to the open market on several occasions.
  2. None of us is guilty.
  3. B, who is a visitor, has been observed at the open market.
  4. All of my statements are false.
- B. 1. A is not the guilty one.
  2. D owns a cart.
  3. I have never been to the open market.
  4. D is a visitor to Athens, but has been here several times.
- C. 1. A's first and third statements are false.
  2. D does not own a cart.
  3. This is D's first visit to the Athens.
  4. B's statements are all true.
- D. 1. I do not own a cart.
  2. B is the guilty one.
  3. This is my first visit to Athens.
  4. B's third statement is true.

Which of the four is guilty?

(Hints on page 44)
(Solution on pages 61–63)

— 2 —

Mordin's Maze

A knight, far from home and seeking shelter in a storm, happened upon what appeared to be an abandoned castle. In reality it was the abode of Mordin the Sorcerer. The knight was received and provided with food and drink containing a potion that rendered him senseless.

When the his head cleared, the knight found that he was in a room in the depths of the castle. His gaze fell on a stone tablet leaning against the nearby wall, with this message:

> You are about to encounter Mordin's Maze. If you wish to be freed, you must make correct judgments as you travel through eight rooms. At each decision point you will find a choice of doors to pass through. You will be guided by a sign on each door. Select the correct one and you will continue on your way through the maze. All other doors lead to dead ends from which there is no escape or return. Be warned: Signs may be true or false.

Since no other option presented itself, the knight was determined to successfully negotiate the maze.

P2-1 The First Choice*

The knight approached two doors at the end of the room and read these signs:

A
| Only one of these signs is false. |

B
| This is the door you should go through. |

Which door should be opened?

(Hints on page 45)
(Solution on page 63)

P2-2 The Second Choice*

Having selected the right door, the knight passed into a second room and found two doors from which to choose. Each contained a sign, as follows:

A
| These signs are both false. |

B
| This is the way to go. |

Which door is the correct one?

(Hints on page 45)
(Solution on page 63)

P2-3 The Third Choice*

Again the knight went through the correct door and entered another room, this time containing a choice of three doors, with these signs:

A | Exactly two of these signs are false.

B | This is the door to go through.

C | Enter the next room through this door.

Which door should be chosen?

(Hints on page 45)
(Solution on page 64)

P 2-4 The Fourth Choice*

Having made the right selection, the knight continued through the maze, and encountered a choice of three doors, with these signs:

A | Do not go through door C.

B | At least one of these signs is false.

C | If door A is not the one to go through, then door B is.

Which is the right choice?

(Hints on page 45)
(Solution on page 64)

P2-5 The Fifth Choice*

Proceeding correctly into the fifth room, the knight perceived three doors. He read their signs, as follows:

A	B
These signs are all false.	The sign on door A is true.

C

This is the correct door to open.

Which door leads to the next choice?

(Hints on page 45)
(Solution on page 65)

P2-6 The Sixth Choice*

Once again, the knight selected the correct door and entered the sixth room, which contained three doors, with these signs:

A	B
No fewer than two of these signs are false.	None of these signs is false.

C

Go through either this door or the door with the sign that is true.

Which door is the one to go through?

(Hints on page 45)
(Solution on page 65)

P2-7 The Seventh Choice*

After taking a deep breath, the knight chose one of the doors and entered the seventh room. He observed four doors, as follows:

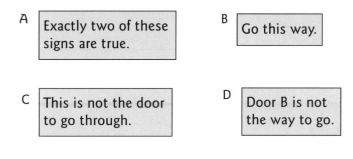

| A Exactly two of these signs are true. | B Go this way. |
| C This is not the door to go through. | D Door B is not the way to go. |

Which door should the knight select?

(Hints on page 45)
(Solution on page 66)

P2-8 The Eighth Choice**

Having successfully passed the first seven decisions, the knight entered the eighth and final room of the maze. He found three doors, with these signs:

| A This is not the door to go through unless the sign on the adjacent door is true. | B Exactly two of these signs are false. |

C This is the door to open unless the sign on the adjacent door is false.

The knight entered the correct door, which opened into a wooded area near the entrance to the castle, where he found his faithful horse awaiting him.

What door was opened?

(Hints on page 45)
(Solution on pages 66–67)

— 3 —

The Isle of Ave

Somewhere in the far and forlorn reaches of the North Sea is the small island of Ave, on which strange things happen. That the island is watched over by Neptune, and that some say it is enchanted, are only part of its uniqueness.

The Isle of Ave is inhabited by an unusual people. Avians have their own standards of veracity.

P3-1 Neptune Establishes Communication*

The inhabitants of the Isle of Ave belong to three groups: Soravians, who always speak truthfully; Noravians, who always speak falsely; and Midravians, who make statements that are alternately truthful and false—in which order is unknown.

Since the Isle of Ave is under his watchful eye, Neptune would like to establish communication with the Avians. To do so, it is necessary to know who has what standard of veracity. He approaches three inhabitants, A, B, and C, known to be a Soravian, a Noravian, and a Midravian, not necessarily in that order. He asks one of them two questions:

Neptune: Are you the Soravian?
    A: No.
Neptune: Is B the Soravian?
    A: No.

Neptune now knows which of the three is the Soravian, which is the Noravian, and which is the Midravian. Do you?

(Hints on page 46)
(Solution on page 67)

P3-2 Two Avians*

Avians belong to three different groups: Soravians, who always speak truthfully; Noravians, who always speak falsely; and Midravians, who make statements that are alternately truthful and false, but not necessarily in that order. The two speakers below are known to belong to different groups.

A. B is a Noravian.
B. A's statement is truthful.

To what groups do A and B belong?

(Hints on page 46)
(Solution on page 68)

P3-3 Umbrellas to Sell*

Since it rains continually on the Isle of Ave, you would think that an umbrella purveyor would find it an ideal place to ply his trade. The problem in dealing with Avians, however, is communication. A visiting seller of umbrellas approaches three Avians and asks which group each represents.

The three are known to be a Soravian, who always speaks truthfully; a Noravian, who always speaks falsely; and a Midravian, who makes statements that are alternately truthful and false, but the order is uncertain. The three make the following statements:

A. C will answer falsely to all questions.
B. A's statement is false.
C. B's statement is false.

Frustrated by his inability to interpret the Avians' statements, the visitor leaves, deciding that it would be best to sell his umbrellas in some other place.

Which one is the Soravian, which one is the Midravian and which one is the Noravian?

(Hints on page 46)
(Solution on page 68)

P3-4 Visit from a Hippogriff*

The Isle of Ave seems to be a stopping place for all manner of strange beasts. There is, however, considerable excitement among the inhabitants, as a hippogriff has visited the island for the first time. This monster has the body of a horse and the wings, head, and talons of an eagle. Three inhabitants are discussing the visitor.

The three are known to be a Soravian, who always speaks truthfully; a Noravian, who always speaks falsely; and a Midravian, who makes statements that are alternately truthful and false, or false and truthful. Their statements follow:

A. 1. I have seen hippogriffs on the island several times.
    2. You cannot believe anything that B says.
B.   A has never seen a hippogriff before.
C.   If A says he has seen hippogriffs on the island before, you can count on it's being true.

Who is the Soravian, who is the Noravian, and who is the Midravian?

(Hints on pages 46)
(Solution on page 69)

23

P3-5 To Catch an Aspidochelon*

The aspidochelon is a sea monster so huge that it resembles an island. However it is rumored to be a gastronomical delicacy. Three Avian fishermen are contemplating an aspidochelon hunt.

Avians belong to three different groups: Soravians, who always speak truthfully; Noravians, who always speak falsely; and Midravians, who make statements that are alternately truthful and false, although not necessarily in that order. As to the three fishermen, little is known as to their group or groups. Their statements follow:

- A. 1. The last time we caught an aspidochelon, C and I helped hold the net.
  - 2. I am a Soravian.
- B. 1. I am not a Midravian.
  - 2. We do not know for sure if aspidochelon is good to eat.
  - 3. A's first statement is false.
- C. 1. None of us has ever seen an aspidochelon.
  - 2. I am a Noravian.

What group or groups do the three fishermen represent?

(Hints on page 46)
(Solution on pages 69–70)

P3-6 Is D Neptune Visiting in Disguise?*

The Avians are watched over by Neptune, who occasionally visits them in disguise. Three Avians are discussing a fourth individual, who may be Neptune in disguise, although there seems to be a difference of opinion.

Inhabitants of Ave are known to be Soravians, who

always speak truthfully; Noravians, who always speak false-ly; or Midravians who make statements that are alternately truthful and false, or false and truthful. The group or groups of the three speakers below are unknown:

A. 1. I saw D suddenly appear from behind a tree.
   2. None of us is a Soravian.
   3. B is a Noravian.
B. 1. D is Neptune visiting us in disguise.
   2. Only one of us is a Soravian.
   3. I am not a Midravian.
C. 1. D is my next-door neighbor.
   2. A is a Soravian, as is D.

What group or groups are represented by the three speakers?

(Hints on page 46)
(Solution on pages 70–71)

P3-7 A's Statement Is Truthful*

Neptune is finding that establishing meaningful dialogue with the Avians is not as easy as he thought it would be. Perhaps he needs to be a little more direct. Neptune steps up to four inhabitants and insists on a truthful statement.

Among the four, at least one is known to be a Soravian, who always speaks truthfully; at least one is known to be a Noravian, who always speaks falsely; and at least one is known to be a Midravian, who makes statements that are alternately truthful and false, but in unknown order. Each makes one statement, as follows:

A. I am either a Soravian, a Noravian, or a Midravian.
B. I am either a Soravian or a Midravian.
C. I am either a Noravian or a Midravian.
D. I am either a Soravian or a Noravian.

Considering that two of the four statements are truthful and two are false, what does Neptune now know about each of the four?

(Hints on page 46)
(Solution on page 71)

P3-8 A Problem with a Sea Monster**

Three Avian fishermen are known to be a Soravian, who always speaks truthfully; a Noravian, who always speaks falsely; and a Midravian, who makes statements that are alternately truthful and false. A sea monster has been caught in their nets and the three are discussing the problem, as follows:

A. 1. This is not the first time the sea monster has gotten caught in our nets.
   2. I am going to change jobs if this does not stop happening.
   3. C speaks truthfully only part of the time.
B. 1. This is the first time a sea monster has gotten caught in our nets.
   2. C was so frightened that he fell overboard.
   3. The sea monster took more fish than we did.
C. 1. A is not going to change jobs if this does not stop happening.
   2. I did not fall overboard.
   3. The sea monster did not take more fish than we did.

Neptune resolved the problem by advising the sea monster to leave the area.

Which is the Soravian, the Noravian, and the Midravian?

(Hints on pages 46–47)
(Solution on page 72)

There Are Outliers

The Avians' unusual standards of veracity are important to the island's traditions. There are a few, however, who do not accept the value of tradition, and who do not observe the conventional island standards of veracity. These are Outliers. How truthful they are is not known, except that their responses are different from those of the Soravians, Noravians, and Midravians.

P3-9 Visitors from the Sea**

Once a year, the Isle of Ave is visited by the Sea People for their special feast day, to which Avians are invited. Four inhabitants are discussing the festivities.

As to the four who make the statements below, one is a Soravian, who always speaks truthfully; one is a Noravian, who always speaks falsely; and one is a Midravian, who makes statements that are alternately truthful and false. The fourth does not follow the customary Avian standards of veracity and must be considered an Outlier.

- A. 1. My statements are not all truthful.
  - 2. We are lucky to be part of the festivities.
  - 3. I find it difficult to relate to these people, with their fins, tails, and scales.
  - 4. I am the Midravian.
- B. 1. I agree with A's third statement.
  - 2. I am doing more than my share helping to get ready for the big feast.
  - 3. My statements are all truthful.

C. 1. My statements are all truthful.
 2. With all these people crowded onto the island it will surely sink.
 3. I am to be the guest of honor at the feast.
 4. We are all overworked.
D. 1. I agree with A's first statement.
 2. C's first statement is truthful.
 3. I am the Midravian.

Which one is the Soravian; which one is the Noravian; which one is the Midravian; and which one is the Outlier?

(Hints on page 47)
(Solution on pages 72–73)

P3-10 Recreational Activities on Ave***

There are four principal recreational activities enjoyed by the inhabitants of Ave: giant sea horse racing, boating, fishing, and swimming. Five Avians are discussing these activities and who enjoys each.

Avians are divided into three groups according to their standards of veracity: Soravians always speak truthfully; Noravians always speak falsely, and Midravians make statements that are alternately truthful and false. There are also those few inhabitants who insist on being different. Their standards of veracity are unlike those of the three traditional groups. They are Ave's Outliers. As to the five who make the statements below, their groups are unknown except that one and only one of them is an Outlier.

A. 1. D enjoys boating.
 2. E enjoys both swimming and fishing.
 3. B is a Soravian.
 4. E is not a Noravian or a Midravian.

B. 1. C enjoys all four recreational activities.
   2. A is not a Midravian.
   3. I agree with D's third statement.
   4. I am a Soravian.
C. 1. B enjoys all four recreational activities.
   2. D has no interest in fishing.
   3. I do not enjoy boating.
   4. E is not a Soravian.
D. 1. I enjoy three recreational activities.
   2. I enjoy boating.
   3. C's recreational interest is limited to fishing.
   4. A's third statement is false.
E. 1. C enjoys giant sea horse racing and swimming.
   2. Two of my recreational activities are giant sea horse racing and boating.
   3. A's recreational activities are limited to giant sea horse racing and boating.
   4. D only enjoys one of the four recreational activities.

What is the standard of veracity of each of the five Avians, and, considering that no two of them have the same number of the four activities, what recreational activities are enjoyed by each?

(Hints on pages 47–48)
(Solution on pages 73–75)

— 4 —

The Villagers of Farmwell

These puzzles involve the activities of the people who inhabited a shire within the kingdom of Lidd.

The puzzles contain statements that provide limited amounts of pertinent information. They afford just enough information for you to arrive at the correct solutions. However, you will find that there is one false statement in each puzzle. To find the correct solution, first determine which statement should be discarded.

P4-1 The Village Fair*

The annual village fair is a much anticipated event, and the livestock showings and awards are an important part of the festivities. This year it was necessary to have four separate showings to accommodate the large number of entries: daybreak to midmorning, midmorning to midday, midday to midafternoon, and midafternoon to sundown. One showing was for cows, one for goats, one for pigs, and one for sheep—not necessarily in that order. The animals winning the four categories were owned by Dor, Edvo, Frer, and Har, and one of their entries won the blue ribbon for best animal in the fair.

Of the six statements that follow, five are valid and one is false. Based on these statements, who owned which animal; what was the showing time for each; and which animal was awarded the blue ribbon?

1. The sheep escaped from its owner shortly after mid-morning and was not recaptured until the next day.
2. Edvo was convinced that his goat would win the blue ribbon.
3. Dor left the show with her entry at midday and did not return.
4. The blue ribbon winner was entered in the midday to midafternoon showing, immediately following the goat's showing.
5. Frer's animal was entered in a later showing than that in which the pig was entered.
6. Edvo's animal was entered in the first showing of the day.

(Hints on page 48)
(Solution on page 75–76)

P4-2 Encounter with the Dragon Meduso*

A comely village lass had been captured by the dreaded dragon Meduso. This dragon was not only large and fierce, with fiery breath, but had the power to turn anyone to stone who looked directly into his eye. The village leaders appealed to the King for knightly assistance to free the lass. Sir Hector, who had the duty that day, set out on his steed.

Sir Hector made four attempts to rescue the village lass. In one attempt, he used his peripheral vision to fight the dragon. However, the smoke and fire from Meduso's breath caused irritation to his eyes and the resulting tears restricted his vision. In another attempt, he used his highly polished shield as a mirror in which to see the dragon, but clouds of smoke from the dragon's breath obscured the reflection. In one attempt, he slipped into the cave at night while the dragon was sleeping. However, the dragon, who was a very light sleeper, awoke and chased Sir Hector from the cave. In another attempt, he blindfolded himself and located the dragon by his sound. However, his lance struck a sturdy oak tree, jolting him from his mount.

As Sir Hector was preparing for a fifth attempt, his squire arrived with the news that the fair damsel had returned, having escaped while the dragon was out foraging for food.

From the following statements, what was the sequence of Sir Hector's four attempts to rescue the village lass? Of the six statements below, five are valid and one is false.

1. At least one other attempt followed Sir Hector's attempt to use his peripheral vision.
2. Sir Hector's attempt to use a blindfold was not immediately before or immediately after the attempt to slip into the cave.
3. The attempt by Sir Hector to slip into the dragon's cave was not his fourth attempt.
4. Sir Hector's attempt to use his polished shield was immediately before his attempt to slip into the dragon's cave.
5. Sir Hector's attempt to use a blindfold was not after his attempt to use his polished shield.
6. Sir Hector's attempt to use his peripheral vision was not immediately before or immediately after his attempt to use a blindfold.

(Hints on pages 48–49)
(Solution on pages 76–78)

P4-3 The Dragon Watch**

Because of the ever present danger of dragons, the villagers took turns keeping watch. During one particular period, five people were assigned watch duty, each on one of five shifts. Their ages varied, with no two being the same age. From the statements below, determine the order in which the watches were held and the relative age of each of the five villagers. One statement below is false; the others are valid.

1. Har was not the oldest, the youngest, nor did he have the first or fifth watch.
2. The youngest of the five, who was neither Edvo nor Tolo, did not have the fifth watch.
3. Winn was younger and had a later watch than Edvo, who stood a later watch and was younger than Frer.
4. Tolo, who was not the second oldest or fourth oldest, was older than Har, and had an earlier watch than Frer.
5. Edvo's relative position in the order of the watches was the same as his relative position in age.
6. Har was next to Tolo in age and next to Edvo in the order of watches held.
7. The fourth oldest held a later watch than Tolo, but an earlier watch than Edvo, who had a later watch and was younger than Frer.
8. The one who held the second watch was the oldest of the five villagers.

(Hints on page 49)
(Solution on pages 78–79)

P4-4 New Ponies**

Ponies were used for labor and were the primary means of transportation in Farmwell. Four villagers, who were neighbors, each recently acquired a pony. One was black; one was palomino; one was gray; and one was white. They varied in height from nine to twelve hands, no two being the same height. The four neighbors were Boro, Jes, Kover, and Tolo. Their second names were Son of Alfo, Son of Dirk, Son of Evel, and Son of Fergy, not necessarily in that order.

From the statements below, determine the first name and second name of each of the four neighbors, and the color and height of the pony each acquired. One of the six statements is false, the rest are valid.

1. Tolo, who lived next to Son of Fergy and across from Son of Evel, did not acquire a pony that was ten hands high, nor was his new pony's color palomino or black; his pony was acquired immediately after Kover's pony.
2. Boro, whose new pony was white, was the second to acquire a pony, followed by Son of Evel, whose pony was not eleven hands high.
3. Son of Dirk's new pony was the second one to be acquired; it was neither nine hands high nor eleven hands high.
4. The last of the four to acquire a pony did not own the one that was eleven hands high.
5. Son of Alfo, who lived next to Kover, acquired a black pony.
6. The neighbor whose new pony was twelve hands high was the first of the four to acquire a pony.

(Hints on page 49)
(Solution on pages 80–81)

P4-5 Work and Recreation**

The villagers were industrious, each working hard at a particular trade. Among five of them, one was a weaver, one was a carpenter, one was a blacksmith, one was a cobbler, and one was a miller.

A happy people, they enjoyed singing, dancing, instrumental music, telling stories, and sharing puzzles. Each had a favorite and a second-favorite activity. Based on the statements below, what was the vocation of each and what was the favorite and second-favorite activity of each? No two had the same favorite and no two had the same second-favorite. One statement below is false; the rest are true.

1. The one whose favorite activity was singing was much in demand because of the simplicity and high quality of the furniture he built.
2. Dancing was the favorite activity of the cobbler.
3. Fram's second-favorite was the same as Dok's favorite; Zett's second-favorite was the same as Winn's favorite.
4. Neither the blacksmith nor the miller enjoyed telling stories.
5. Winn, who was not the miller, enjoyed storytelling most; his second-favorite activity was dancing.
6. The weaver enjoyed instrumental music most; his second-favorite activity was singing.
7. The cobbler, Hober, and the miller were good friends.
8. The second-favorite activity of the carpenter was storytelling.

(Hints on page 50)
(Solution on pages 81–82)

P4-6 A Giant in the Shire***

The villagers were fortunate that relatively few monsters or other adversaries invaded their shire. When a giant looking for an easy meal began stealing livestock, a group of the people united and, presenting a formidable presence, were successful in driving the giant away. Among those in the group were Alf, Bord, Dek, Fober, and Hon. Their second names were Son of Edno, Son of Lor, Son of Quin, Son of Rup, and Son of Tas. Their occupations were as follows: two raised sheep, one raised cattle, one raised goats, and one raised pigs. In chasing the giant away, two wielded pitchforks, one wielded an ax, one wielded a club, and one wielded a spade.

From the statements that follow, what was the first name and second name of each of the five; what was the occupation of each; and what weapon was wielded by each? Of the seven statements, one is false, the rest are valid.

1. Neither Son of Rup nor Son of Tas, both of whom wielded pitchforks, raised sheep or goats.
2. Dek, Hon (who raised cattle), Alf (who was not Son of Rup), and Son of Tas were among the leaders in organizing the group to attack the giant.
3. Son of Edno and Son of Quin raised sheep.
4. Dek, who was not Son of Tas, and Fober, who wielded a spade, had adjacent farms.
5. Although Son of Quin was reluctant, at the last minute he was persuaded by Son of Edno and Alf to join the group.
6. Son of Lor did not raise goats or pigs.
7. Alf, who did not raise sheep, wielded an ax.

(Hints on page 51)
(Solution on pages 83–85)

P4-7 Pony Races***

The most important sporting events in the shire were pony races. In one series of four races, six riders competed. No rider won more than one race. From the statements below, what was the ranking of each rider in each race? ("Before" means in a higher-ranking position, not necessarily immediately before; "after" means lower-ranked, not necessarily immediately after.) Of the sixteen statements, fifteen are valid and one is false.

1st race
1. Pro finished before Pen, who finished before Ismo.
2. Lak finished before Pro.
3. Pir finished after Ismo.
4. Adus finished in third place.

2nd race
5. Lak finished before Ismo, who finished before Adus.
6. Pro finished in the same place as in the previous race.
7. Pir finished in fifth place.
8. Pen finished before Lak.

3rd race
9. Pen finished before Pro, who finished before Pir.
10. Pir finished after Lak and before Ismo.
11. Lak finished before Pen.
12. Pir did not finish in the same place as he did in either of the first two races.

4th race
13. Pir finished one position better than his best position in any of the other three races.
14. Pro finished before Adus and after Lak.
15. Pen finished in fifth place.
16. Lak finished after Pir.

(Hints on page 51)
(Solution on pages 85–86)

— 5 —

The Valley Liars

Among strange lands, the Land of Liars is unparalleled. The inhabitants all make false statements. However, they adhere to definite patterns according to the time of day. There are those who speak the truth in the morning and lie in the afternoon. The inhabitants in this group are known as Amtrus. There are also those who speak the truth in the afternoon and lie in the morning. The inhabitants in this group are known as Pemtrus.

There is a valley in the Land of Liars, in which the inhabitants have their own patterns of veracity: The Amtrus are like others in the Land except that in any statements specifically mentioning other Amtrus they lie in the morning and tell the truth in the afternoon. The Pemtrus are like other Pemtrus in the Land except that in any statements specifically mentioning other Pemtrus they lie in the afternoon and tell the truth in the morning.

To solve each puzzle, you must determine which speakers are Amtrus and which are Pemtrus, and whether it is morning or afternoon.

P5-1 A Visitor to the Land of Liars*

A traveler enters the Land of Liars intending to visit the Valley of Liars. He is aware that Amtrus speak the truth in the morning and lie in the afternoon, and that Pemtrus speak the truth in the afternoon and lie in the morning. The visitor encounters two inhabitants. He inquires as to the time of day and as to the group or groups to which the two belong. They reply as follows:

A.   B and I are Pemtrus.
B. 1. A is not a Pemtru.
    2. It is either morning or afternoon.

Is it morning or afternoon; and to what group or groups do the two inhabitants of the Land of Liars belong?

(Hints on page 52)
(Solution on page 87)

P5-2 En Route to the Valley of Liars*

Still heading toward the Valley of Liars, the visitor approaches a fork in the road. One road leads north and the other east. Two inhabitants are asked for directions. The two reply as follows:

A. 1. Take the road leading east.
    2. It is morning.
B. 1. Take the road leading north.
    2. I am an Amtru.

Which road should the visitor take?

(Hints on page 52)
(Solution on pages 87–88)

P5-3 Two Valley Liars*

The visitor reaches the Valley of Liars. He has been advised that they have their own patterns of veracity. They are like others in the Land of Liars except that when Amtrus specifically mention other Amtrus they lie in the morning and speak the truth in the afternoon; and when Pemtrus specifically mention other Pemtrus they lie in the afternoon and speak the truth in the morning.

Two Valley inhabitants are asked the time of day and to what group or groups they belong. They respond as below:

A. B and I are Pemtrus.
B. A is not a Pemtru.

Is it morning or evening; and to what group or groups do the two Valley inhabitants belong?

(Hints on page 52)
(Solution on page 88)

P5-4 Two More Valley Liars*

Two Valley inhabitants, A and B, are asked to what group or groups they belong. They respond as follows:

A. 1. B is a Pemtru.
    2. B and I belong to the same group.
B.   A's statements are false.

Is it morning or afternoon; and to what group or groups do A and B belong?

(Hints on page 52)
(Solution on pages 88–89)

P5-5 Three Valley Liars**

The statements below are made by three Valley inhabitants, whose group or groups are unknown.

A. If asked, B would erroneously claim that he and I belong to the same group.
B. If you ask C the time of day, he will say it is morning.
C. A's statement is false.

Is it morning or afternoon; and to which group does each of the three speakers belong?

(Hints on page 52)
(Solution on pages 89–90)

P5-6 Three Valley Liars Again**

Three Valley inhabitants make statements. As to their group or groups, little is known.

A. C and I are not both Pemtrus.
B. C and I belong to the same group.
C. A and I do not belong to the same group.

Is it morning or afternoon; and to which group does each belong?

(Hints on page 52)
(Solution on pages 90–91)

P5-7 Four Valley Liars**

Four Valley inhabitants make the following statements. Of these four, little is known as to their group or groups.

A. If you were to ask D, he would say that I am a Pemtru.

B. I am the only one from my group.
C. If asked, B would claim that he and I belong to the same group.
D. B and I are Amtrus.

Is it morning or afternoon; and to which group or groups do the four Valley inhabitants belong?

(Hints on page 52)
(Solution on pages 91–92)

P5-8 Who Is the Impostor?***

Of the five individuals who make the statements below, one is a visitor from another land and not subject to the Valley standards of veracity. He is an impostor, posing as an inhabitant. As to the four inhabitants, Amtrus and Pemtrus are equally represented.

A. C and I do not belong to the same group.
B. It is either afternoon, or else I am a Pemtru.
C. A is not a Pemtru.
D. Either A is an Amtru, or else I am an Amtru.
E. It is either afternoon, or else I am an Amtru.

Which speaker is the impostor; is it morning or afternoon; and what group is represented by each of the four inhabitants?

(Hints on page 52)
(Solution on pages 92–93)

HINTS

H1 SOCRATES LENDS A HAND

Diagrams will be helpful in solving these puzzles. List the speakers on one axis and the statement numbers on the other, as below.

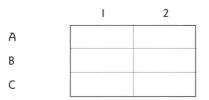

Assume that each speaker in turn affords the correct solution, and mark T or F as you form conclusions.

H1-1 Who Owns the Mule? Consider that each farmer made one true and one false statement. Review A's statements. Could A be the owner?

H1-2 Theft of Homer's Writings Consider that each suspect made one true and two false statements. Review A's statements assuming that B is guilty. Could B be guilty?

H1-3 Who Left the Cell Door Open? Consider that among the four guards, three of their statements are true, and five of their statements are false. If A is guilty, how many true statements are there?

H1-4 A Secret Observer Consider that all statements are true except any mentioning the secret observer. Consider A's and B's statements. Could A be the observer?

H1-5 Theft from the Statue of Athena Consider that one suspect made three true statements, and one suspect made three false statements. Which one of the four suspects made three true statements?

H1-6 Who Should Lead the Victory Parade? Consider that one soldier made one false statement; one made two false statements; and one made three false statements. Assume that A should lead the parade. If so, is this consistent with the statements made by the three speakers?

H1-7 Socrates Plans a Trip Consider that the disciple selected made either three true or three false statements. Of the other two, one made two true and one false statement, and one made one true and two false statements. Consider C's statements. Could C be the disciple selected?

H1-8 Who Should Repair the Statue? Consider that each of the craftsmen made the same number of true statements. Assume that A is the most qualified. If so, do all four have the same number of true statements?

H1–9 Who Won the Discus Throw? Consider that no two made the same number of true statements. Can you determine which one made three true statements?

H1-10 The Food Produce Thief Consider that the one who delivered the milk made three true statements; the one who delivered the cheese made two true statements; the one who delivered the honey made one true statement; and the one who delivered the bread and the one who delivered the nuts each made no true statements. What can you determine from A's and D's first statements?

H1-11 Theft at the Open Market Consider that since none of the suspects is completely truthful, one made three true statements, one made two true statements one made one true statement, and one made no true statements. What can you conclude from A's fourth statement? How about A's second statement?

H2 MORDIN'S MAZE

For each of these puzzles, one of the signs makes a statement about the truthfulness or falseness of the group of signs. In each case, consider the possibility of the sign being true or false. In determining the solution, be sure that the answer is conclusive.

For puzzles **2-1** and **2-2**, the following diagram is suggested:

	sign A	sign B
if door A	T	F
if door B	T/F	T

For puzzles **2-3**, **2-4**, **2-5**, **2-6**, and **2-8**, add door and sign C to your diagram.

H2-1 The First Choice Could sign B be true?

H2-2 The Second Choice Could sign A be true?

H2-3 The Third Choice Could sign A be false?

H2-4 The Fourth Choice Could sign B be false?

H2-5 The Fifth Choice Could sign A be true?

H2-6 The Sixth Choice Could sign B be true?

H2-7 The Seventh Choice The diagram below is suggested: Consider the implications of sign C being true.

	sign A	sign B	sign C	sign D
if sign A is true				
if sign A is false				

H2-8 The Eighth Choice Consider that the sign on door B is true. How about if it is false?

Prepare a diagram such as the following and enter '+' or '−' as you formulate conclusions regarding the group of each speaker:

	Sor	Nor	Midr
A			
B			
C			

H3-1 Neptune Establishes Communication Could A be a Soravian? How about a Noravian?

H3-2 Two Avians Consider that the two speakers belong to two different groups. Could B's statement be truthful? If not, why not?

H3-3 Umbrellas to Sell Consider C's response to A's statement. What does it tell you?

H3-4 Visit from a Hippogriff What is wrong with A's first statement? What does it tell you about C's statement?

H3-5 To Catch an Aspidochelon Consider that the group or groups represented are unknown. Could C's statement be truthful? What are the possibilities for B?

H3-6 Is D Neptune Visiting in Disguise? Again the group or groups represented are unknown. Consider C's second statement and A's second statement. What can we say about C?

H3-7 A's Statement Is Truthful A key to this puzzle is that two of the four statements are truthful and two are false. Consider C's statement; is it truthful or false?

H3-8 A Problem with a Sea Monster Consider A's third statement. If it is truthful, what does that say about the standards of veracity of the three Avians? Are their statements consistent?

Puzzles **3-9** and **3-10** contain the additional complication of an Outlier. To be different, an Outlier must make at least two consecutive statements that are both truthful or both false and at least one statement that is false or truthful, not necessarily in that order.

H3-9 Visitors from the Sea Prepare a diagram, as below:

	Sor	Nor	Mid	Out
A				
B				
C				
D				

We can conclude that A's first statement is truthful. What does that say about A's other three statements?

H3-10 Recreational Activities on Ave The following diagram will be helpful:

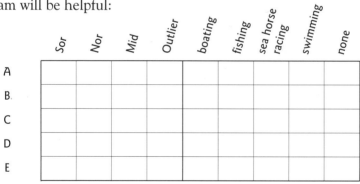

	Sor	Nor	Mid	Outlier	boating	fishing	sea horse racing	swimming	none
A									
B									
C									
D									
E									

No two of the five Avians have the same number of the four principal activities. Therefore, we can conclude that one enjoys four activities, one enjoys three, one enjoys two, one enjoys one, and one enjoys none of the four activities.

Compare A's first statement and D's second statement. Also compare A's third statement and D's fourth statement. What do these comparisons tell you?

H4 THE VILLAGERS OF FARMWELL

For these puzzles, it is suggested that the reader analyze the statements in each, considering that they are valid until a contradiction appears. Careful review at this point will identify possible invalid statements, and provide a basis for determining the false one.

H4-1 Village Fair Construct a diagram, such as below. Mark a plus or minus sign as you confirm or reject a conclusion:

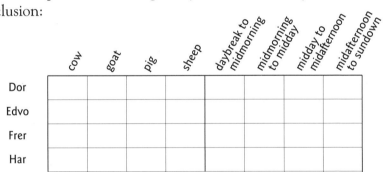

Consider statement 1. What showing for the sheep is indicated?

H4-2 Encounter with the Dragon Meduso Prepare a diagram, such as below:

	blindfold	vision	shield	cave
first				
second				
third				
fourth				

Consider statements 1, 3, 4, and 5. Can you determine which encounter was fourth?

H4-3 The Dragon Watch Prepare a diagram, as below:

	Assigned Watch					youngest	4th oldest	3rd oldest	2nd oldest	oldest
	1st	2d	3rd	4th	5th					
Edvo										
Frer										
Har										
Tolo										
Winn										

Consider statements 1, 3, and 4. What relative age for Winn is indicated? Is this consistent with statement 2?

H4-4 New Ponies Prepare a diagram, such as the following. Enter the requested information as you determine it.

first name	second name	size	color	order of acquisition
Boro				
Jes				
Kover				
Tolo				

Although the order of acquisition is not requested in the solution, it is helpful in analyzing the required information.

From statements 1 and 5, if true, what was Tolo's second name?

H4-5 Work and Recreation Two diagrams, such as those following, will be helpful:

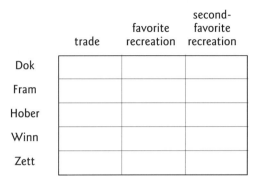

	trade	favorite recreation	second-favorite recreation
Dok			
Fram			
Hober			
Winn			
Zett			

trade	favorite recreation

Consider statements 1, 2, and 6; if true, what are the two possibilities as to the villager who enjoyed storytelling most?

H4-6 A Giant in the Shire A composite diagram, such as the one shown here, will be helpful.

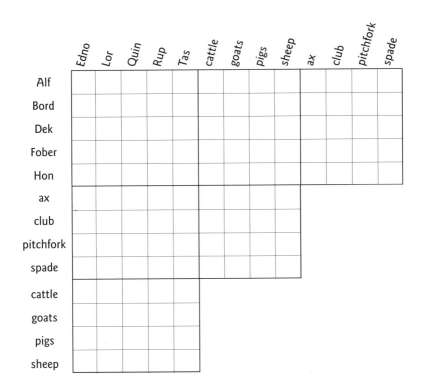

From statement 1, if true, what were the occupations of the two villagers who wielded pitchforks?

H4-7 Pony Races For this puzzle, list the riders in each race generally in the order in which they finished and readjust the rankings until there is no conflict.

H5 THE VALLEY LIARS

For each puzzle, prepare a diagram indicating Amtru and Pemtru on one axis and listing each speaker on the other axis. Assume either morning or afternoon and test the consistency of the statements against your assumption. As you test your assumptions, look for contradictions.

H5-1 A Visitor to the Land of Liars What does B's second statement tell us about B? How about A?

H5-2 En Route to the Valley of Liars What can we conclude from A's second statement? What about B's second statement?

H5-3 Two Valley Liars If it is morning, could A's statement be true? What about B's statement?

H5-4 Two More Valley Liars Is this puzzle essentially the same as the previous one? If not, why not? Test A's first statement against the possibility of it being afternoon.

H5-5 Three Valley Liars Consider A's statement. What are the possibilities for A and B?

H5-6 Three Valley Liars Again Consider A's statement. What are the possibilities for A?

H5-7 Four Valley Liars What do we know from B's statement? Consider the possibilities and compare them to D's statement and its possibilities.

H5-8 Who Is the Impostor? Consider B's statement? What are the possibilities? Also consider that there are two Amtrus and two Pemtrus.

SOLUTIONS

S1-1 Who Owns the Mule?

CONSIDERATIONS

Consider that each farmer made one true and one false statement.

	1	2
A	F	T
B	T	F
C	F	T

Assume that A is the owner. If so, both of A's statements are false. Therefore, A is not the owner. Assume that C is the owner. If so, both of C's statements are true. Therefore, C is not the owner. Therefore, B is the owner.

SUMMARY SOLUTION   It is B's mule.

S1-2 Theft of Homer's Writings

CONSIDERATIONS

Assume B is guilty. If so, A's second and third statements are true. Therefore, B did not do it. Assume C is guilty. If so, B's first and second statements are true. Therefore, C did not do it. Therefore, A is guilty.

	1	2	3
A	F	T	F
B	T	F	F
C	F	T	F

SUMMARY SOLUTION   A is the thief.

S1-3 Who Left the Cell Door Open?

CONSIDERATIONS

Consider that three statements are true, and five are false.

Assume that A is guilty. If so, A's first and second statements are both false; B's statements are both true; C's first statement is false, and second is true; and D's first statement is true, and second is false. Therefore, since, if A did it, there are four true statements, A is not guilty.

Assume that B is guilty. If so, A's first statement, C's first and second statement, and D's first statement are true. Therefore, B did not do it.

Assume that C is guilty. If so, A's first and second statement, B's first statement, C's second statement, and D's first statement are true. Therefore, D did not do it. By elimination, D is guilty.

	1	2
A	T	F
B	T	F
C	F	T
D	F	F

SUMMARY SOLUTION   D is guilty.

S1-4 A Secret Observer

CONSIDERATIONS

Assume A is the observer. If so, A's statements are true. C's second statement, which refers to A, confirms A's second statement. Therefore, A is not the observer. Also, in confirming A's second statement, C's second statement verifies that D is not the observer.

Assume C is guilty. If so, A's first statement, which refers to C, must be false. However, D's second statement confirms A's first statement. Therefore, C is not the observer. Therefore, D's first statement, which claims C's first statement is false, is true. B is the observer.

	1	2
A	T	T
B	T	T
C	F	T
D	T	T

SUMMARY SOLUTION   B is the observer.

S1-5 Theft from the Statue of Athena

CONSIDERATIONS

Consider that one suspect made three true statements.

A's second statement is false, as it was given that all four suspects were in Athens when the crime occurred. C's second statement is false, as there was evidence that the thief acted alone. From D's first statement, we know that at least one of D's statements is false. Therefore, B is the one with three true statements.

From B's third statement, C was seen at the Acropolis late that night. This agrees with D's second statement. Therefore, since we know that at least one of D's statements if false, D's third statement must be false. D did it.

	1	2	3
A	T	F	F
B	T	T	T
C	F	F	F
D	T	T	F

SUMMARY SOLUTION   D is the thief.

S1-6 Who Should Lead the Victory Parade?

CONSIDERATIONS

Consider that one made one false statement, one made two false statements, and one made three false statements.

Assume that A should lead the parade. If so, A's first two statements are true. Therefore, A's third statement must be false. If so, C's third statement must be true, and C must be the one with one true statement. Therefore, C's second statement must be false. Therefore, B's third statement must be true. Therefore, since each soldier would have at least one true statement, A is not the correct choice.

Assume that B should lead the parade. If so, B's first two statements are true and third statement must be false. Therefore C's second statement must be true. Therefore C's third statement must be false. This means that A's third statement must be true. Again, each soldier would have at least one true statement.

Therefore, C is the correct choice. A has made three false statements; B has made two false statements; and C has made one false statement.

	1	2	3
A	F	F	F
B	F	F	T
C	T	F	T

SUMMARY SOLUTION
C should lead the parade.

S1-7 Socrates Plans a Trip

CONSIDERATIONS

Consider that the disciple Socrates selects made three true or three false statements. One of the other two made two true and one false statement. The remaining one made one true and two false statements.

C's first and third statements are contradictory. One is true and one is false. Therefore, C is not the one who is selected.

Assume that B is selected. If so, C is the one with two true statements, and A has made one true statement, either his first or second one. However, A's first and second statements contradict B's third and first statements. One of A's two statements and one of B's statements must be true. Therefore, since B's second statement is false, B is not the one with three true or three false statements. B was not selected.

A is the disciple selected. C has made one true statement, and B is the one with two true statements. Since B's second statement is false, his first and third statements are true; and A's three statements are false.

	1	2	3
A	F	F	F
B	T	F	T
C	F	F	T

SUMMARY SOLUTION
Socrates selects A.

S1-8 Who Should Repair the Statue?

CONSIDERATIONS
Consider that each of the four craftsmen made the same number of true statements and the same number of false statements.

Assume that A is the most qualified. If so, B has at least two true statements; and each of the other three has at least two false statements. Therefore, A is not the most qualified.

Assume that B is the most qualified. If so, A's and C's first and third statements are consistent. However their second statements are not. Therefore, each of these two has a different number of true statements. Therefore, B is not the most qualified.

Assume that D is the most qualified. If so. D's first the third statements are false, D's second and A's first statements agree, and A's second statement is true. Therefore, A and D each has a different number of true statements. Therefore, D is not the most qualified.

C is the most qualified. A's first and second statements are false, and third statement is true; B's first and second statements are false, and third statement is true; C's first statement is true, and second and third statements are false; D's first statement is true, and second and third statements are false.

	1	2	3
A	F	F	T
B	F	F	T
C	T	F	F
D	T	F	F

SUMMARY SOLUTION
C is the most qualified.

S1-9 Who Won the Discus Throw?

CONSIDERATIONS
Since no two made the same number of true statements, it is apparent that one made three true statements, one made two true statements, one made one true statement, and one made no true statements.

Assume that A was the winner. If so, only A's first statement and B's first statement confirm this. B must be the one with all true statements, since, if A was the winner, his second statement is false. If so, B was second and B and C trained together; A's third statement is false; D's first and third statements are false, and second statement is true. Therefore, A and D would each have made only one true statement. Therefore, A was not the winner.

Assume that C was the winner. If so, D must be the one with all true statements. If so, B was second, and C and D trained together. If so, A's three statements and C's three statements are false. Therefore, C was not the winner.

Assume that D was the winner. If so, either A or D could be the one with three statements. Assume it is A. If so, A was second, and A and C trained together. If so, both C and D would each have made only one true statement. Therefore, if D was the winner, A was not the one with three true statements.

Assume D was the winner, and D was the one with three true statements. If so, B was second, and C and D trained together. If so, A and B have each made only one true statement. Therefore, D was not the winner.

Therefore, B was the winner; C was the one with all true statements; A was second; and C did not train with anyone.

	1	2	3
A	T	T	F
B	F	F	F
C	T	T	T
D	T	F	F

SUMMARY SOLUTION
B was the winner.

S1-10 The Food Produce Thief

CONSIDERATIONS

Consider that the one who delivered the milk made three true statements; the one who delivered the cheese made two true statements and one false statement; the one who delivered the honey made one true and two false statements; the one who delivered the nuts, and the one who delivered the bread, each made three false statements.

A is the one who delivered the bread and D is the one who delivered the nuts. We know this, since the two who delivered these two food products made only false statements, and neither B, C, nor E could have delivered the bread or nuts as the first statement or statements would be true. A and D, who each accuse the other, are both innocent.

E's first statement must be true, since it would be false only if made by the citizen who delivered the milk, and that citizen made three true statements. Therefore E must be the one who delivered the goats' cheese, or the one who delivered the honey. If E is the one who delivered the honey, his second and third statements must be false. However, since we know E's third statement to be true, E is the one who delivered the cheese. E's second statement must be false. Therefore, C is not the thief. Since we know that D is not the thief, C's third statement is true. C is either the one who delivered the milk or the one who delivered the honey.

Our conclusions at this point are:

	1	2	3	delivery
A	F	F	F	bread
B				
C			T	
D	F	F	F	nuts
E	T	F	T	cheese

If C is the one who delivered the milk, from C's second statement B is guilty. If C is the one who delivered the honey, C's first and second statements are false, and B is innocent. From A's third statement, which we know to be false, B did not deliver the honey. Therefore, B, whose statements are all true, delivered the milk; C, whose first and second statements are false, delivered the honey; and E is the thief.

SUMMARY SOLUTION

A. bread
B. milk
C. honey
D. nuts
E. cheese; E is the thief.

S1-11 Theft at the Open Market

CONSIDERATIONS

Since none of the suspects is completely truthful, and no two suspects made the same number of true statements, we can conclude that one made three true statements, one made two true statements, one made one true statement, and one made no true statements.

A's fourth statement is false as, if it were true, it would be a contradiction. Therefore, A made at least one true statement. A's second statement is clearly false, as it was a given that one of the four is guilty. Therefore, either or both of A's first and third statements must be true.

D's second and fourth statements are contradictory: either one is true and one is false, or both are false. If D's third statement is true, A's first statement is false and his third statement must be true. However, this makes D's fourth statement false. If A's first statement is true, D's third statement is false. Therefore, either D's third or fourth statements are false, or both are false.

C's first statement is false, as either or both of A's first and third statements must be true. Also, C's fourth statement is false, as none of the four suspects is completely truthful.

The suspect with no true statements must be B, C or D. Assume that B is the suspect with no true statements. If so, B's first statement is false and A is guilty. If so, D's second statement claiming B is guilty must be false. Since we know that either or both of D's third and fourth statements are false, D has made at least two false statements. Since either B or D must be the suspect with three true statements (A and C each have made at least two false statements), we can eliminate B as the suspect with no true statements.

Therefore, the suspect with no true statements must be either C or D. Since C's second statement and D's first statement both agree, they must both be false. Since C's third statement and D's third statement agree, they must also be false. Therefore, C is the suspect with no true statements.

Our conclusions, so far:

	1	2	3	4
A		F		F
B				
C	F	F	F	F
D	F		F	

We know that D's first and third statements are false. Since we know that either D's second or fourth statements are false, D must be the suspect with one true statement, and B is the suspect with three true statements.

Therefore, A is the suspect with two true statements, the first and third ones. Therefore, since D's fourth statement disagrees with A's third statement, which is true, D's only true statement is the second one, B is guilty.

SUMMARY SOLUTION
B is guilty.

S2-1 The First Choice

CONSIDERATIONS
The sign on door A must be true. There is no way of validating sign A's statement as false. The sign on door B must be the false one. Door A is the correct door.

	sign A	sign B
if door A is correct	T	F
if door B is correct	T/F	T

SUMMARY SOLUTION
Door A is the one to go through.

S2-2 The Second Choice

CONSIDERATIONS
The sign on door A must be false. For it to be true would be a contradiction. Therefore, the sign on door B is true. Therefore, door B is the correct choice.

	sign A	sign B
if door A	F/T	F
if door B	F	T

SUMMARY SOLUTION
Door B is the one to take.

S2-3 The Third Choice

CONSIDERATIONS

If door B is the correct door, the sign on door B is true and the sign on door C is false. This means that the sign on door A is false, making that sign true, a contradiction. If door C is the correct door, the sign on door C is true and the sign on door B is false. Again, the sign on door A presents a contradiction. Door A is the correct choice.

	sign A	sign B	sign C
if door A	T	F	F
if door B	T/F	T	F
if door C	T/F	F	T

SUMMARY SOLUTION
Door A is the correct one to take.

S2-4 The Fourth Choice

CONSIDERATIONS

The sign on door B must be true. Therefore, either or both of the signs on doors A and C are false. If door A is the one to go through, the signs at both doors A and C are true. If door B is the one to go through, the signs on doors A and C are, again true. Therefore, Door C is the correct choice.

	sign A	sign B	sign C
if door A	T	T/F	T
if door B	T	T/F	T
if door C	F	T	F

SUMMARY SOLUTION
Door C is the right choice

S2-5 The Fifth Choice

CONSIDERATIONS

The sign on door A must be false. If it were true, it would be a contradiction. Since the sign on door B agrees with the sign on door A, it is also false. Therefore, the sign on door C is true, and door C is the way to go.

	sign A	sign B	sign C
if door A	F	F	F
if door B	F	F	F
if door C	F	F	T

SUMMARY SOLUTION
Door C is the right door.

S2-6 The Sixth Choice

CONSIDERATIONS

The sign at door B must be false, since it disagrees with the sign at door A, and claims no false signs. The sign on door A must be true, since if it were false, it would represent the second false sign, and validate its statement. Therefore, the sign on door C is the second false sign. (Note: Door A cannot be the way to go as the sign on door C agrees with this, and sets up a contradiction which is not resolved by the sign on door A being determined to be false.) Therefore, from C's false statement, door B is the way to go.

	sign A	sign B	sign C
if door A	T	F	T/F
if door B	T	F	F
if door C	T	F	T/F

SUMMARY SOLUTION
Door B is the one to take.

S2-7 The Seventh Choice

CONSIDERATIONS

Assume the sign on door A is true. If so, since the signs at doors B and D disagree, one of them must be false, and the sign on door C must be the second false sign, in which case, the sign on door D is true. Assume the sign on door A is false. If so, again, since the signs at doors B and D disagree. one of them must be false. If the sign on door A is false, there must be an additional false sign, the sign on door C; and the sign on door D is true.

In either case, the sign on door C is false; door C is the correct choice.

	sign A	sign B	sign C	sign D
if sign A is true	T	F	F	T
if sign A is false	F	F	F	T

SUMMARY SOLUTION
Door C should be selected.

S2-8 The Eighth Choice

CONSIDERATIONS

Assume that the sign on door B is true. If so, the sign on door A is false, and is the wrong choice. If so, the sign on door C is false, and it also is the wrong choice. In this case, B is the door to take.

If the sign on door B is false, the signs on doors A and C must both be true. (If one of A and C were true and the other false, along with the false sign on door B the sign on door B would be true—a contradiction.) In this case as well, door B is the correct choice.

Regardless of whether the sign at door B is true or false, door B is the way to go. Consider both alternatives:

	sign A	sign B	sign C
if door A	F	T	F
if door B	F	T	F
if door C	F	T	F

	sign A	sign B	sign C
if door A	T	F	T
if door B	T	F	T
if door C	T	F	T

SUMMARY SOLUTION

B is the correct door.

S3-1 Neptune Establishes Communication

CONSIDERATIONS

A must be the Midravian. Only a Midravian could answer "no" to the question, "Are you the Soravian?" A Soravian, who always speaks truthfully, would answer "yes;" a Noravian, who always speaks falsely, would also answer "yes."

Since A's first response was truthful, his second response is false; B is the Soravian and C is the Noravian.

	Sor	Nor	Mid
A	–	–	+
B	+	–	–
C	–	+	–

SUMMARY SOLUTION   A.   Midravian
                                        B.   Soravian
                                        C.   Noravian

S3-2 Two Avians

CONSIDERATIONS

B's statement must be false, since if truthful, it would confirm that B is a Noravian. A truthful statement would not be possible for a Noravian. B is a Midravian. Since the two represent different groups, A, whose statement is false, is a Noravian.

	Sor	Nor	Mid
A	–	+	–
B	–	–	+

SUMMARY SOLUTION A. Noron
B. Midron

S3-3 Umbrellas to Sell

CONSIDERATIONS

If C were the Noravian or the Soravian, A's statement would be denied, as Noravians always speak falsely and Soravians always speak truthfully. Therefore, C is the Midravian. A, who has made a false statement, is the Noravian and B is the Soravian.

	Sor	Nor	Mid
A	–	+	–
B	+	–	–
C	–	–	+

SUMMARY SOLUTION A. Noravian
B. Soravian
C. Midravian

S3-4 Visit from a Hippogriff

CONSIDERATIONS

C's statement infers that A is the Soravian. If true, C is the Midravian and B is the Noravian. However, it was given that this was the first visit from a hippogriff. Therefore, both C's statement and A's first statement are false. Therefore, B is the Soravian, and, from A's second statement, which is false, A is the Noravian and C is the Midravian.

	Sor	Nor	Mid
A	–	+	–
B	+	–	–
C	–	–	+

SUMMARY SOLUTION   A. Noravian
                                 B. Soravian
                                 C. Midravian

S3-5 To Catch an Aspidochelon

CONSIDERATIONS

C's second statement is false, since it claims that C is a Noravian. If true, it would be impossible, as Noravians always speak falsely. Therefore, C must be a Midravian, and his first statement is true.

Therefore, A's first statement is false, since it is contradicted by C's first statement. Therefore, A's second statement is also false. A must be a Noravian.

Since we know A's first statement to be false, B's third statement, which confirms this, is true. Therefore, B's first statement must also be true. Therefore, since B is not a Midravian, he must be a Soravian.

	Sor	Nor	Mid
A	–	+	–
B	+	–	–
C	–	–	+

SUMMARY SOLUTION   A. Noravian
                   B. Soravian
                   C. Midravian

S3-6 Is D Neptune Visiting in Disguise?

CONSIDERATIONS

C's second statement is false, since it claims A is a Soravian, which A's second statement denies. Therefore, neither A nor C is a Soravian.

If A's second statement is truthful, he is a Midravian and his third statement is false. If so, at least one of B's statements is truthful. If B's third statement is truthful, B must be a Soravian. If so, this refutes A's second statement. If B's second statement is truthful, B must be a Soravian, since we know that neither A nor C is a Soravian. Therefore, A's second statement is false. One of the three speakers is a Soravian, and, again, it must be B.

Since A's third statement is refuted, A is a Noravian. Since B's first statement refutes C's first statement, C is a Noravian.

	Sor	Nor	Mid
A	–	+	–
B	+	–	–
C	–	+	–

SUMMARY SOLUTION A. Noravian
                  B. Soravian
                  C. Noravian

S3-7 A's Statement Is Truthful

CONSIDERATIONS

A's statement is truthful, since each of the three possibilities is covered. A is either a Soravian or a Midravian, since a Noravian can not speak truthfully. C's statement must be truthful, as it could be false only if C were a Soravian, and a Soravian can not make a false statement. C must be a Midravian, as a Noravian can not make a truthful statement.

Therefore, B and D are the two who have made false statements. B must be a Noravian, as the statement would be truthful for either a Soravian or a Midravian

D must be a Midravian, as the statement would be true if made by a Soravian or a Noravian. Therefore, A must be the Soravian.

	Sor	Nor	Mid
A	+	−	−
B	−	+	−
C	−	−	+
D	−	−	+

SUMMARY SOLUTION A. Soravian
                  B. Noravian
                  C. Midravian
                  D. Midravian

S3-8 Problem with a Sea Monster

CONSIDERATIONS

If A's third statement is truthful, C is the Midravian, A must be the Soravian, and B must be the Noravian. If so, C's first statement must be false, since it contradicts A's second statement. If so, C's second statement is truthful and third statement is false. However, C's third statement contradicts B's third statement. One is truthful and the other is false. Therefore, A's third statement must be false. Therefore, A's first statement is also false. The Soravian is either B or C. B's first statement contradicts A's first statement. Therefore, B's first statement is truthful.

Conclusions at this point are:

	Sor	Nor	Mid
A	–		
B		–	
C			

Since B's first statement is truthful, his third statement, which contradicts C's third statement, is also truthful. C is not the Soravian. Therefore, B is the Soravian; C, who has made three false statements, is the Noravian; A, whose first and third statements are false and second statement is truthful, is the Midravian.

SUMMARY SOLUTION   A.   Midravian
                                B.   Soravian
                                C.   Noravian

S3-9 Visitors from the Sea

CONSIDERATIONS

A's first statement must be true. It would be true for anyone but a Soravian, and this would be impossible as Soravians always speak truthfully. A is not the Soravian or the Noravian. A could be a Midravian, but, if so, the fourth statement must be false, because if A were a Midravian, the first and third statements would be true, and the second and fourth statements would be false. Therefore, A is not the Midravian; A is the Outlier.

D's first statement, which agrees with A's truthful first statement, is truthful. Therefore, D's third statement is also truthful. D is the Midravian.

At this point our conclusions are:

	Sor	Nor	Mid	Out
A	–	–	–	+
B			–	–
C			–	–
D	–	–	+	–

D's second statement must be false. C is not the Soravian; C must be the Noravian, and B is the Soravian.

SUMMARY SOLUTION   A. Outlier
                    B. Soravian
                    C. Noravian
                    D. Midravian

S3-10 Recreational Activities on Ave

CONSIDERATIONS

Since no two of the five enjoy the same number of the four recreational activities, it is apparent that one enjoys four activities, one enjoys three activities, one enjoys two activities, one enjoys one activity, and one enjoys none of the four activities.

A's first statement and D's second statement agree. They are either both truthful or both false. A's third statement and D's fourth statement are contradictory. One is truthful and one is false. One of these two is the Outlier.

B's first statement, indicating that C enjoys all four activities, is inconsistent with B's third statement, which agrees with D, that C's interest is limited to one activity. Therefore, since both statements cannot be truthful, they must both be false. Therefore B's fourth statement, claiming to be a Soravian, is also false. B is a Noravian. Therefore, B's second statement, indicating that A is not a Midravian, is false. A is a Midravian. Therefore, D is the Outlier. A's first and third statements are false, and second and fourth statements are truthful. D's second statement is false and fourth statement is truthful.

A's fourth statement, which is truthful, indicates that E is not a Noravian or a Midravian. Since D is the Outlier, E must be a Soravian. C's fourth statement, that E is not a Soravian, is false. Therefore, C's second statement is also false. A's second statement, which is truthful, indicates that E enjoys both swimming and fishing. E's second statement, which is also truthful, claims giant sea horse racing and boating. Therefore, E is the one with all four recreational activities. Therefore, C's first statement that B enjoys all four recreational activities is false. C is a Noravian. At this point our conclusions are:

	Sor	Nor	Mid	Out	boating	fishing	sea horse racing	swimming	none
A	−	−	+	−					
B	−	+	−	−					
C	−	+	−	−					
D	−	−	−	+					
E	+	−	−	−	+	+	+	+	

C's third statement falsely claims not to enjoy boating. E's first statement indicates that C enjoys giant sea horse racing and swimming. Therefore, C enjoys boating, giant sea horse racing, and swimming. C's second statement, which is false, indicates that D has no interest in fishing. E's truthful fourth statement indicates that D enjoys only one of the four principal recreational activities. Therefore, D's sole activity is fishing.

A's two recreational activities, as indicated by E's third statement, are sea horse racing and boating. Therefore, B must be the one with none of the four principal activities.

SUMMARY SOLUTION

A. Midravian — giant sea horse racing, boating
B. Noravian — none
C. Noravian — giant sea horse racing, boating, and swimming
D. Outlier — fishing
E. Soravian — giant sea horse racing, boating, fishing, and swimming

S4-1 The Village Fair

CONSIDERATIONS

Statement 1 suggests that the sheep must have won in the daybreak to midmorning showing. From statement 6, Edvo's animal was entered in the daybreak to midmorning showing. From these two statements we would conclude that Edvo's animal was the sheep. However, statement 2 indicates that Edvo's animal was the goat. Therefore, the false statement is either 1, 2, or 6. From statement 4, the goat's showing must have been from midmorning to midday. Therefore, the false statement must be either 2 or 6.

From statements 1 and 3, Dor, who did not own the sheep, must have won the midmorning to midday showing.

From statement 4, Dor's animal is the goat. Therefore, the false statement is 2. From statement 6, Edvo's animal is the sheep.

Conclusions at this point are:

	cow	goat	pig	sheep	daybreak to midmorning	midmorning to midday	midday to midafternoon	midafternoon to sundown
Dor	−	+	−	−	−	+	−	−
Edvo	−	−	−	+	+	−	−	−
Frer		−		−	−	−		
Har		−		−	−	−		

From statements 4 and 5, Frer's animal, the cow, was entered in the mid-afternoon to sundown showing; Har's animal, the pig, was entered in the midday to mid-afternoon showing, and from statement 4, was the blue ribbon winner.

SUMMARY SOLUTION

Dor   goat   midmorning to midday
Edvo   sheep   daybreak to midmorning
Frer   cow   midafternoon to sundown
Har   pig   midday to midafternoon (blue ribbon winner)

S4-2 Encounter with the Dragon Meduso

CONSIDERATIONS

From statement 1, Sir Hector's attempt to use his peripheral vision was not his fourth one. From statement 3, the attempt by Sir Hector to slip into the dragon's cave was not his fourth one. From statements 4 and 5, we can conclude that neither the attempt to use his polished shield nor the attempt to use a blindfold was the fourth one. Since one of these four attempts had to be the fourth one, it is apparent that one of statements 1, 3, 4, and 5 must be the false one.

Assume that statement 3 is the false statement. If so, from statements 4 and 5, the attempt to use the polished shield was the third attempt and the blindfold was either the first or second attempt, as was the attempt to use peripheral vision. However, from statement 6, the blindfold and peripheral vision attempts were not in consecutive order. Therefore, statement 3 is not the false one.

Assume that statement 4 is the false one. If so, from statement 5, the blindfold attempt was before the polished shield attempt; and from statements 1 and 6, the peripheral vision attempt must have followed the polished shield attempt, leaving the attempt to slip into the cave as the fourth one. However, from statement 2, this was not the case. Therefore, statement 4 was not the false one.

Assume that statement 5 is the false statement. If so, from statement 4, the polished shield attempt was immediately before the attempt to slip into the cave. If so, from statements 1 and 6, the peripheral vision attempt must have been the first, and the blindfold attempt the fourth one. However, from statement 2, the blindfold attempt did not immediately follow the attempt to slip into the cave. Therefore, statement 5 is not the false one. Therefore, statement 1 is the false statement.

Therefore, from statements 5 and 4, the blindfold attempt was first, followed by the polished shield attempt, then the attempt to slip into the cave. The fourth attempt was the peripheral vision one.

	blindfold	vision	shield	cave
first	+	–	–	–
second	–	–	+	–
third	–	–	–	+
fourth	–	+	–	–

First:	blindfold
Second:	polished shield
Third.	slip into cave
Fourth:	peripheral vision

S4-3 The Dragon Watch

CONSIDERATIONS

From statement 1, Har was not the youngest. From statement 3, neither Edvo nor Frer was the youngest. From statement 4, Tolo was not the youngest. Therefore, if these statements are true, Winn must be the youngest. Also from statements 1, 3, and 4, Winn held the fifth watch. However, from statement 2, Win could not have held the fifth watch and be the youngest. One of these statements must be false.

Assume that statement 1 is false. If so, Har could be either the youngest or have held the fifth watch. However, from statements 4 and 6, Har was not the youngest, and from statements 3 and 6, Har did not hold the fifth watch. Therefore, the false statement is not statement 1.

Assume that statement 3 is false. If so, Edvo could be either the youngest or have held the fifth watch, as could Frer. However, from statement 2, Edvo was not the youngest, and from statements 7 and 5, since he was younger than Frer, he did not hold the fifth watch. From statement 6, Frer was neither assigned a later watch nor was he younger than Edvo. Therefore, statement 3 is not false.

Assume that statement 4 is false. If so, Tolo could have stood the fifth watch or be the youngest. However, from statement 2, Tolo was not the youngest, and from statement 7, he was not the tallest. Therefore, the false statement is statement 2.

Therefore, Winn stood the fifth watch. Har did not stand the first watch, and Tolo stood an earlier watch than Frer or Edvo. Tolo stood the first watch. Since Har was not the oldest, from statement 8, he was not assigned the second watch. Therefore, Frer, who stood an earlier watch than Edvo (statement 3), stood the second watch and, from statement 8, was the oldest.

From statements 4 and 7, Tolo was not the second oldest, the fourth oldest or the youngest. Therefore, Tolo was the third oldest. Also from statement 7, Edvo was not the fourth oldest or the youngest. Therefore, Edvo was the second oldest. Since the fourth oldest stood an earlier watch than Edvo, Har must have been the fourth oldest and Winn was the youngest. Since the fourth oldest stood an earlier watch than Edvo, Har had the third watch and Edvo had the fourth watch.

	Assigned Watch					youngest	4th oldest	3rd oldest	2nd oldest	oldest
	1st	2d	3rd	4th	5th					
Edvo	−	−	−	+	−	−	−	−	+	−
Frer	−	+	−	−	−	−	−	−	−	+
Har	−	−	+	−	−	−	+	−	−	−
Tolo	+	−	−	−	−	−	−	+	−	−
Winn	−	−	−	−	+	+	−	−	−	−

SUMMARY SOLUTION

Edvo	fourth watch	second oldest
Frer	second watch	oldest
Har	third watch	fourth oldest
Tolo	first watch	third oldest
Winn	fifth watch	youngest

CONSIDERATIONS

From statement 1, Tolo was not Son of Fergy or Son of Evel. From statements 1 and 5, since Tolo's new pony was not black, he was not Son of Alfo. Therefore, if both statements 1 and 5 are true, Tolo was Son of Dirk.

However, statements 2 and 3 indicate that Boro was second to acquire a new pony, as was Son of Dirk. Either Tolo was not Son of Dirk, or Boro was not second to acquire a pony, or Son of Dirk was not second to acquire a pony.

From statements 2 and 4, if both are true, Boro's pony must have been eleven hands. From statement 3, if true, Son of Dirk's new pony was not eleven hands. Therefore, the false statement must be 2, 4, or 3.

Therefore, statements 1 and 5 are true; Tolo was Son of Dirk. From statements 1 and 6, Tolo's pony was not ten or twelve hands. Therefore, it was nine or eleven hands. Therefore, statement 3, which states that Son of Dirk's pony was neither nine hands nor eleven hands, is false.

Therefore, Boro was the second to acquire a pony. From statement 1, since Tolo's pony was acquired immediately after Kover's, Tolo was the fourth to acquire a pony, Kover was third, and Jes was first.

From statements 2 and 5, Boro, who acquired the white pony, was the Son of Fergy, and Jes was the Son of Alfo. His pony was black.

From statement 4, Tolo did not acquire the pony that was eleven hands. Therefore, Tolo's pony was nine hands. From statement 2, Kover, Son of Evel, whose pony was not twelve hands or eleven hands, acquired the pony that was ten hands. Boro, whose pony was not twelve hands, acquired the pony that was eleven hands; Jes's pony was twelve hands.

Conclusions, so far:

first name	second name	size	color	order of acquisition
Boro	Son of Fergy	11	white	2nd
Jes	Son of Alfo	12	black	1st
Kover	Son of Evel	10		3rd
Tolo	Son of Dirk	9		4th

From statement 1, Tolo's pony was not palomino; it was gray, and Kover's was palomino.

SUMMARY SOLUTION

Boro	Son of Fergy	eleven hands	white
Jes	Son of Alfo	twelve hands	black
Kover	Son of Evel	ten hands	palomino
Tolo	Son of Dirk	nine hands	gray

S4-5 Work and Recreation

CONSIDERATIONS

From statement 1, the carpenter's favorite activity was singing. From statement 2, the cobbler's favorite activity was dancing. From statement 6, the weaver enjoyed instrumental music most. Therefore, either the blacksmith or the miller must have enjoyed storytelling most. However, from statement 4, neither enjoyed storytelling. Therefore, the false statement must be 1, 2, 4, or 6.

From statement 5, Winn was not the cobbler or the miller. From statement 8, he was not the carpenter or the weaver. (From statement 5, his second-favorite activity was dancing.) Therefore, Winn was the blacksmith, and, from statement 5, he enjoyed storytelling most. Therefore, statement 4 is the false one.

Conclusions at this point are, as follows:

	trade	favorite recreation	second-favorite recreation		trade	favorite recreation
Dok					blacksmith	stories
Fram					cobbler	dancing
Hober					carpenter	singing
Winn	blacksmith	stories	dancing		miller	
Zett					weaver	instrum.

The miller's favorite activity must have been puzzles

From statements 3 and 8, Zett, whose second favorite was storytelling, was the carpenter. From statement 7, Hober was the weaver. From statement 6, his second favorite was singing.

From statement 3, since Fram's second favorite, which was not dancing (it was Winn's), was the same as Dok's favorite, Dok was not the cobbler. Therefore, Fram was the cobbler and Dok was the miller. Fram's second favorite was puzzles, and Dok's favorite activity was also puzzles. Fram's favorite activity was dancing and Dok's second favorite was instrumental music.

SUMMARY SOLUTION

name	trade	favorite recreation	second-favorite recreation
Dok	miller	puzzles	instrumentals
Fram	cobbler	dancing	puzzles
Hober	weaver	instrumentals	singing
Winn	blacksmith	story telling	dancing
Zett	carpenter	singing	storytelling

CONSIDERATIONS

From statements 2, and 5, Alf was not Son of Rup, Son of Tas, Son of Quin, or Son of Edno. Therefore, if the two statements are valid, Alf's second name was Son of Lor.

From Statement 6, Son of Lor did not raise goats or pigs. Therefore, if true, he must have raised cattle or sheep. However, from statement 7, Alf did not raise sheep, and from statement 1, he must have raised goats. (Since neither of the two who wielded pitchforks raised sheep or goats, one raised cattle and the other raised pigs.) Therefore, either Alf was not Son of Lor, in which case, either statement 2 or statement 5 is false; or Alf did not raise goats, in which case either statement 1 or statement 7 is false; or Son of Lor raised goats, in which case, statement 6 is false.

Assume that statement 2 is false. If so, this statement does not validate that Alf was not Son of Rup or Son of Tas. However, from statement 1, both wielded pitchforks, and from statement 7, Alf wielded an ax. Therefore, statement 2 is not false.

Assume that statement 5 is false. If so, Alf could be either Son of Edno or Son of Quin. However, from statement 7, Alf did not raise sheep, and from statement 3, both Son of Edno and Son of Quin raised sheep. Therefore, statement 5 is not false. Therefore Alf was Son of Lor.

From statement 6, if true, Son of Lor must have raised sheep or cattle. However, from statement 7, Alf did not raise sheep (which is validated by statement 3) or cattle (which is validated by both statements 1 and 2). Therefore, statement 6 is the false statement. Therefore, Alf raised goats.

From statement 1, Son of Rup and Son of Tas raised cattle and pigs. From statement 2, Hon, who was not Son of Tas raised cattle. Therefore, Hon was Son of Rup, and Son of Tas raised pigs. Both wielded pitchforks. From statement 3, Son of Edno and Son of Quin raised sheep.

Our conclusions, so far, are:

	Edno	Lor	Quin	Rup	Tas	cattle	goats	pigs	sheep	ax	club	pitchfork	spade
Alf	−	+	−	−	−	−	+	−	−	+	−	−	−
Bord		−		−		−	−			−			
Dek		−		−		−	−			−			
Fober		−		−		−	−			−			
Hon	−	−	−	+	−	+	−	−	−	−	−	+	−
ax	−	+	−	−	−	−							
club		−		−	−	−							
pitchfork	−	−	−	+	+	−							
spade		−		−	−	−							
cattle	−	−	−	+	−								
goats	−	+	−	−	−								
pigs	−	−	−	−	+								
sheep	+	−	+	−	−								

From statements 2 and 5, since Dek was one of the leaders in organizing the group, he was not Son of Quin, and, from statement 4, he was not Son of Tas. Therefore, Dek was Son of Edno. Also from statement 4, since Fober wielded a spade, Dek wielded a club. Since Bord must have wielded a pitchfork, he was Son of Tas, and Fober was Son of Quin.

SUMMARY SOLUTION

Alf Son of Lor	goats	ax
Bord Son of Tas	pigs	pitchfork
Dek Son of Edno	sheep	club
Fober Son of Quin	sheep	spade
Hon Son of Rup	cattle	pitchfork

S4-7 Pony Races

CONSIDERATIONS

1ST RACE

From statements 2 and 1, Lak finished before Pro, who finished before Pen and Ismo, and, from statement 4, Adus
finished in third place. From statement 3, Pir must have finished in sixth place. Therefore, if statements 1, 2, 3, and 4
are valid, Lak was first, pro was second, Adus was third, Pen
was fourth, Isom was fifth, and Pir was sixth.

2ND RACE

From statements 6 and 7, if valid, Pro finished in second
place and Pir finished in fifth place. In the four remaining
places, from statements 5 and 8, if valid, Pen was first, Lak
was third, Ismo was fourth, and Adus was sixth.

3RD RACE

From statements 9 and 11, if valid, Lak was second (He was
not first, since he won the 3rd race and no rider won more
than one race.), Pen was third, and Pro was fourth. From
statement 10, if valid, Pir was fifth and Ismo was sixth.
Adus, who was not named in these statements, was first.

However, statement 12 presents a contradiction, since
from the existing statements Pir finished in fifth place in
both the 2nd and 3rd races. Therefore, either statement 12
is false, or one of the statements placing Pir in fifth place in
either the second or third race is false.

From statements 14, 15, and 16, since Pir finished ahead of Lak, Pen, Pro, and Adus, he must have finished in first or second place. However, from statement 13, his position in either the second or third race must have been second or third. Therefore, statement 12 is not the false statement.

Assume that statement 9 (3rd race) is the false statement. If so, from statements 10 and 11, Pir could not have finished in second or third place. Therefore, statement 9 is not the false one.

Assume that statement 10 is the false statement. If so, from statements 9 and 11, again, Pir could not have finished in second or third place.

Assume that statement 11 is the false statement. If so, from statements 9 and 10, Pir could not have finished in second or third place.

Therefore, the false statement is one describing the finish in the second race, and is clearly statement 7. Therefore, the second race was won by Pen; Pro finished in second place; Pir finished in third place; and Lak, Ismo, and Adus finished in fourth, fifth, and sixth places.

Therefore, in the fourth race, Pir was second, Lak was third, Pro was fourth, Pen was fifth, Adus was sixth, and Ismo was first.

SUMMARY SOLUTION

	Race 1	Race 2	Race 3	Race 4
1.	Lak	Pen	Adus	Ismo
2.	Pro	Pro	Lak	Pir
3.	Adus	Pir	Pen	Lak
4.	Pen	Lak	Pro	Pro
5.	Ismo	Ismo	Pir	Pen
6.	Pir	Adus	Ismo	Adus

S5-1   A Visitor to the Land of Liars

CONSIDERATIONS

From B's second statement we know immediately that it is true. Therefore, B's first statement is also true; A is not a Pemtru. A is an Amtru who has spoken falsely. Therefore, it must be afternoon. Therefore, since B's statement is true, B is a Pemtru.

SUMMARY SOLUTION:

	A	B
Amtru	+	−
Pemtru	−	+

It is afternoon; A is an Amtru; B is a Pemtru.

S5-2 En Route to the Valley of Liars

CONSIDERATIONS

From A's second statement, we can conclude that A is an Amtru. Only an Amtru, true or false, can say it is morning. If it is morning, a Pemtru would lie, saying it is afternoon. If it is afternoon, a Pemtru would truthfully say so. From B's second statement we can conclude that it is morning, whether the statement is true or false. If it were afternoon, a Pemtru would speak the truth, and an Amtru would claim to be a Pemtru. Therefore, A's second statement is true, it is morning, and it follows that his first statement must also be true; the road leading East is the correct one.

Since B disagrees, B must be a Pemtru, in the morning, falsely claiming to be an Amtru.

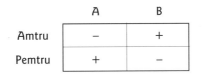

	A	B
Amtru	−	+
Pemtru	+	−

SUMMARY SOLUTION

The road leading East is the correct one. It is morning; A is an Amtru; B is a Pemtru.

S5-3 Two Valley Liars

CONSIDERATIONS

Assume it is morning. If so, A's statement could be true. If so, A and B would both be Pemtrus. B's statement, however, that A is not a Pemtru, would be false—not possible for a Valley Pemtru referring to an inhabitant in the same group in the morning. If it is morning, assume that A is a Pemtru and B is an Amtru. Again, however, B's statement would not be possible, since B would be an Amtru in the morning referring to an inhabitant not in the same group and, therefore, would have to be truthful. The other possibility, that A is an Amtru and B is a Pemtru, could not be made by A, who would have to speak the truth.

Therefore, it is afternoon. A must be an Amtru, since the statement could not be made by a Valley Pemtru in the afternoon. If B is also an Amtru, A would have to truthfully state so. Therefore, B is a Pemtru. B's statement, that A is not a Pemtru, is true.

	A	B
Amtru	+	−
Pemtru	−	+

SUMMARY SOLUTION

It is afternoon; A is an Amtru, and B is a Pemtru.

S5-4 Two More Valley Liars

CONSIDERATIONS

Assume it is afternoon. If so, if A is a Pemtru, his first statement could not be made. A would deny that B is a Pemtru. If it is afternoon, A must be an Amtru. If so, if B were a Pemtru, A would falsely claim that B is an Amtru. If B were an Amtru, A would truthfully confirm this.

Therefore, it is morning. Assume A is an Amtru. If so, if B is an Amtru, A's first statement is false, which is consistent for a Valley Amtru in the morning. However, A's second statement, implying that A and B are both Amtrus would be true, which is an impossible assertion for a Valley Amtru in the morning. If A is an Amtru, B must be a Pemtru, which would be consistent with his first statement. However, A's second statement would be false, which is not consistent.

Therefore, A is a Pemtru. If B were a Pemtru, he would confirm A's statements. Since he rejects them, B is an Amtru, who has told the truth.

	A	B
Amtru	−	+
Pemtru	+	−

SUMMARY SOLUTION
It is morning; A is a Pemtru; B is an Amtru.

S5-5 Three Valley Liars

CONSIDERATIONS
Assume it is morning, and assume A is a Pemtru. If so, A's statement could not be made (If B were a Pemtru, A would confirm it; if B were an Amtru, A would falsely infer that B and he belong to the same group.).

If it is morning, A must be an Amtru. If so, if B were an Amtru, his statement would be true, making C an Amtru. (If C were a Pemtru, B would truthfully indicate that C would claim it is afternoon.) This is not a possible statement for an Amtru to make in the morning, referring to another Amtru.

Therefore, if it is morning, and if A is an Amtru, B must be a Pemtru. If so, if C were an Amtru, B's statement would be true, not a possible statement for a Pemtru in the morning. If C were a Pemtru, B would speak truthfully, indicating that C would claim it is afternoon.

Therefore, it is afternoon. Assume A is an Amtru. Again, A's statement could not be made. (If B were an Amtru, A would confirm it; if B were a Pemtru, A would falsely indicate that B and he belong to the same group.)

Therefore, A is a Pemtru, who has spoken truthfully. B is an Amtru, who has also spoken truthfully. C is an Amtru, whose statement about a Pemtru (A) is false.

	A	B	C
Amtru	−	+	+
Pemtru	+	−	−

SUMMARY SOLUTION
It is afternoon; A is a Pemtru; B and C are Amtrus.

S5-6 Three Valley Liars Again

CONSIDERATIONS
From A's statement, we can conclude that, if it is morning, A must be an Amtru who has spoken truthfully, since a Pemtru in the morning would speak truthfully referring to another Pemtru, falsely if referring to an Amtru. If it is afternoon, A must be a Pemtru, who has spoken truthfully about an Amtru, or falsely about another Pemtru.

From B's statement, we can conclude that B is either an Amtru in the afternoon or a Pemtru in the morning. If B's statement is true, C belongs to the same group. If B's statement is false C is either an Amtru in the morning or a

Pemtru in the afternoon.

From C's statement, we can conclude that C is either an Amtru in the morning or a Pemtru in the afternoon.

Therefore, if it is morning, A has spoken truthfully about another Amtru. However, an Amtru in the morning mentioning another Amtru would not tell the truth. Therefore, it is not morning; it is afternoon.

B, whose statement is false, is an Amtru, and C is a Pemtru. From A's statement, we can conclude that A is a Pemtru, who has made a false statement about two Pemtrus.

	A	B	C
Amtru	−	+	−
Pemtru	+	−	+

SUMMARY SOLUTION
It is afternoon; A and C are Pemtrus; B is an Amtru.

S5-7 Four Valley Liars

CONSIDERATIONS
Assume it is afternoon. If so, if B's statement is true; B is the only Pemtru. If so, D's statement must be false, and D must be an Amtru. If so, A must be an Amtru, and his statement, referring to another Amtru, would have to be true. However, A's statement would be false, an inconsistency.

Therefore, if it is afternoon, B's statement is false; B must be an Amtru. If so, from D's statement, D is an Amtru, since, in the afternoon, a Pemtru referring to an Amtru would speak truthfully. If so, A's statement could not be made. If A were an Amtru, in the afternoon, referring to another Amtru, his statement would have to be true. If A were a Pemtru, in the afternoon, again, his statement would have to be true. In either case, D would not refer to A as a Pemtru.

Therefore, it is morning. Assume that B's statement is false. If so, B is a Pemtru. If so, D, whose statement is false, must also be a Pemtru. However, in the morning, a Pemtru mentioning another Pemtru must speak truthfully.

Therefore, B's statement is true; B is the only Amtru. D's statement is false, and D is a Pemtru. A is also a Pemtru, whose statement regarding D is true. C is also a Pemtru, whose statement referring to an Amtru is false.

	A	B	C	D
Amtru	−	+	−	−
Pemtru	+	−	+	+

SUMMARY SOLUTION
It is morning. A, C, and D are Pemtrus; B is an Amtru.

S5-8 Who is the Impostor?

CONSIDERATIONS
Consider B's statement. The implication is that if it is afternoon, he is an Amtru; if it is morning he is a Pemtru. If it is afternoon, B must be an Amtru who has spoken truthfully. However, in the afternoon, an Amtru would speak falsely, and for the statement to be false, B would be a Pemtru. In the afternoon, a Pemtru would speak truthfully. In either case that would be an impossibility. If it is morning, B must be either a Pemtru, who has spoken truthfully, or an Amtru, who has spoken falsely, again, an impossibility. Therefore, whether it is morning or afternoon, B's statement is not possible. Therefore, B must be the impostor.

Consider that Amtrus and Pemtrus are equally represented.

Assume that it is morning. If so, C's statement could not be made. If C were an Amtru, the inference that A is an

Amtru would have to be false, making A a Pemtru; however, if A were a Pemtru, C would speak truthfully and confirm it. If C were a Pemtru, the statement, referring to an Amtru in the morning would not be possible. If A were an Amtru, C would falsely refer to A as a Pemtru. If A were a Pemtru, C would truthfully indicate so.

Therefore, it is afternoon. A's statement could only be made by a Pemtru (If A were an Amtru he would claim the same group as C, whether true or false.). C's statement is false; it could be made by an Amtru or a Pemtru.

Since we know that A is a Pemtru, if D were an Amtru, his statement would be true, not possible for an Amtru in the afternoon. Therefore, D is a Pemtru, who has spoken falsely about another Pemtru in the afternoon.

If E's statement is true, E is a Pemtru; if it is false he is an Amtru. Therefore, since there are two Amtrus, we can conclude that C and E are both Amtrus who have spoken falsely.

	A	B	C	D	E
Impostor	–	+	–	–	–
Amtru	–	–	+	–	+
Pemtru	+	–	–	+	–

SUMMARY SOLUTION
B is the impostor. It is afternoon; A and D are Pemtrus; C and E are Amtrus.

Index

About the Author

NORMAN D. WILLIS is a retired management consultant. He lives on a lake in the foothills of Washington State's Olympic Mountains, where he spends much of his time fly-fishing. Mr. Willis's other books are *Amazing Logic Puzzles* and *Tricky Logic Puzzles*, both published by Sterling.